I continue to be amazed by Mark's ability to look at everyday situations we all find ourselves in from time to time, and develop them in such a way to make them understandable in a manner that we can relate, learn and profit from. Appreciate and admire your perseverance in putting your thoughts to paper and sharing them. I'm one of those "someday I'll write a book" guys. You are an inspiration.

Jim Weber, Founder and CEO of Wyvern
Technologies, Inc., Silver Star Recipient

Transitions are hard, school. college, jobs, marriage, children. Divorce, retirement or medical conditions. "What comes Next?" offers opinions to help adjust, adapt think and overcome obstacles. Your future will survive.

Steve Amos Engineer, Author

During this time of change, we can count on Mark to help us navigate our way. Great read, Mark!

Bart Zandbergen, Founder
of the Zandbergen Group,
Awarded best -in-State Wealth
management 2020 as published in Forbes

My husband and I have been honored to be included in all the three *American Dream* series books.

Dad, you have been able to capture our journey in a way that makes us so proud of the choices we've made to prosper and thrive in this world of transition. Thank you for highlighting so many unconventional paths and bringing new perspectives to light! I know these books will be beneficial to the many people that read them.

Marias Fierle Hamvey, Television Program Director
Dr. Steven Hamvey, Motion Chiropractic, Austin, TX

Mark has created another winner with down to earth advice on how to live a good, productive life. His stories will inspire people to be their best no matter the situation they find themselves in.

Lee Pound
The Write Coach
Author, Book editor and designer

What Comes Next?

Key strategies and tactics to help deal
with Change, Self-Image, and Self-Esteem

Mark Fierle

What Comes Next

First edition printed December 2020
Published by Solutions Press

ISBN: 978-0-9996497-8-7

Printed in the United States of America

This is a work of non-fiction. The ideas presented are those of the author alone. All references to possible results discussed in this book relate to specific past examples and are not necessarily representative of any future results specific individuals may achieve.

Table of Contents

Foreword

It's been a few years since I started to think about this current book.

It started when I was around quite a few college students and college grads while as a talk show host.

It was obvious so many grads and students had no idea of what they were going to do with their lives after graduating and getting on as responsible adults.

Tell you the truth, don't know if I was any different at that stage of life. Although I do know what I didn't want to do.

What I do know now is that none of us really know what comes next!

Since then I've asked the same questions of many at different stages of their life. That is youths, middle aged and even senior citizens.

Young people trying to figure it out, my suggestion is reading my book *Unbridling the American Spirit*, especially the chapter on "I've got a degree and can't get a job!" Maybe it's not the job or career you want, especially if you have a degree and are tired of flipping hamburgers.

It provides some (if I say so myself) important guidelines to getting on the right track. Most important, don't depend on a college guidance counselor until you have thoroughly vetted them and know their agenda.

Next, we will get into those with life experiences outside of school. This refers primarily to those that have been in the workforce for a time and still can't figure it out or don't feel a degree of satisfaction.

Think about it. If you are near or over 50 and not somewhat satisfied, do you think that will change at the current rate you are going?

By now you have obligations, maybe or probably a family. Hopefully, this short book will give you ideas that will help get you where you can be the best you can be.

There are alternatives and it's up to you to find them. Be in control of your destiny.

Now you have reached what many consider the "Golden years." Hopefully, you have figured it out through trial and error and how you wish the next third of your life to go forward. And that is the key, look forward not backwards.

After all we don't want to be considered an old fogey.

While writing it has been a real pleasure to introduce John Pedroarena and the lessons he has been so generous to share. These in the chapters he provided including Toll Collector, Brainwashing 101 and Denial. I hope John will take these and the others he shared with me and make them into a NY Times bestseller.

Introduction

My objective in this short book is to give my readers some thoughts, ideas, and tips to help with transitions that come their way. Believe me if you live long enough there will be plenty.

I don't consider myself a guru or expert in this area, just using my real-life experiences as well as research I encountered when first deciding to embark on writing of this nature. It's been quite a venture.

I'll share a few examples based on real life and research.

One prime example comes from my time as a radio talk show host. Our show was at the public radio station located at The University of California, Irvine, KUCI 88.9 FM. This gave me the opportunity to interact with many undergrad and graduate students along with others who had their own careers but also had a radio show with either unusual music themes or public interest programs.

Early on in training we were taught by a grad student how to operate the equipment, record programs and other tech types of things. This gal was a young graduate and very bright. One morning a couple of years later she filled in for the host who followed our program.

She called the station and asked if I could fill in for her for about thirty minutes as she would be late. Of course, I did as it was always fun to do this and I could be my version of "Cousin Brucie" (many of you know Cousin Brucie as a prominent DJ from the 60's and 70's eras. He still has a great 60's program on Sirius radio). I used my discretion to play whatever music I wanted. My primary playing was from the great award-winning

Country Blues songwriter Donnie Haddock and his Tramp Iron Railroad Band. I especially like one of his songs entitled, "My wife ran off with the trashman, I don't care about her but, who's going to take out my trash?"

Also told some interesting stories to the audience along the way.

When she finally arrived, I started a conversation about what she was currently taking in her classes.

She mentioned that she received her Degree in Psychology and was now in the process of getting her Masters in the same field.

Of course, nosey me asked what she would do when she completed the Degree. I was dumbfounded when she said she didn't know!

Now I knew she was smart, just didn't know how to go about making a transition. It seems this is not unusual in today's world.

Over the next few years, I made it a habit to ask both students and others similar questions. It was very enlightening how just about everyone had trouble with transition. More examples will be forthcoming.

"Floating like a feather all over the place, never knowing where you are going..." as said in the Forrest Gump movie.

Does this sound like anyone you know? Believe me most of us are like this. Doesn't matter if you are graduating from high school or retiring after working for fifty years. Change is always difficult no matter the age.

It seems that transitioning from one portion of our lives to another is both a time of elation and a time that we say, "Okay, what now?"

It's like going from the known to the unknown. For many it is stressful. We'll talk about that. A career counseling friend of mine used to tell me all the time that most people follow what others in their scope of life do in their career. If their father or maybe their grandfather was a doctor, they focus on becoming a doctor, nurse or somewhere in the medical field. How about if their father was a coal miner, they become a coal miner. In New York City, many Irish become firemen as well as police officers. Why? Because that's their family tradition. Farmers beget farmers, accountants beget accountants, nurses beget nurses, military begets military etc. etc.

Fortunately, in today's world we are open to a plethora of info and some of this traditional stuff is going by the wayside.

As for me, I'm always interested in what people have in mind at all stages of their lives, whether this be after graduating from high school, preparing for college, getting a job, moving from one job to another or getting ready to hang up their spikes as old baseball players do and so forth.

Recently I've heard asked and been asked, "What do you think comes next?"

This from many different people.

One of the most unusual was from a computer tech guy in India who learned I was in the career business and expressed an interest in starting his own business. The problem was he had no idea of what kind of business or what it would take to get a business started.

Now how in the heck would I know what's happening in India?

Here's how I handled it. Not having a ready answer, I said, "What do you really like to do?" and "Can you make a living doing it?"

Of course, there is much more to it than that, at least I gave him something to think about if he was serious.

It was interesting as he also said that while he makes good money now as a tech, he just can't seem to get ahead. I asked, "Why?"

He said, "I get some money, then I spend it."

Here is what I suggested. Most people do the same thing, that's why they don't change and ultimately end up not achieving what they hoped. The way to ensure you achieve what you desire is to pay yourself first and play later. This can be money, education, and experience in your desired field. Make a plan that you can achieve, then stick to it, no matter what. Figure out what you need, how long it will take and go for it.

The object is to pay yourself first and play later, rather than play first and pay later as the old Mastercard ad promoted. Hope he took my advice. Self-image has a great impact on what comes next.

Part I

Making Life's Changes Work

Self-Image

How about people that changed the world without being an expert in that field? There are many, dating back to Louis Pasteur. He was not an MD, just a biologist. However, he was instrumental in developing vaccinations that are instrumental in ridding our world today of deadly viruses. Wish he had been around in our time. As I sit here today the world is experiencing a worldwide pandemic. Don't know how it will end but, it can't be good and may change the world. Then pasteurization. Amazing huh?

Madam Curie also was not an MD but a physicist/chemist. Her research developed Radiology (radium, x-rays) and led to two Nobel prizes (physics and chemistry). How important is that in today's world of medicine?

Then there were the Wright Brothers, not aeronautical engineers but bicycle mechanics. Where would our transportation and airplane industries be today without them?

We can go on and on but let's consider some modern people who changed our world without having a college degree. How important is a college degree when there are so many alternatives, such as trade school? Too bad our schools have basically eliminated trade schools as a viable profession.

Bill Gates is a good example with Microsoft. No, he did not have a college degree and today is one of the richest people in the world. Also, one of the most influential, especially in technology.

Mark Zuckerburg, no college degree but does Facebook care?

What Comes Next?

Steve Jobs was another, he was even fired but the MAC, IPAD, etc. made him unforgettable.

Do you think self-image made a difference in their lives? How important is our own self-image in what we do with our lives? Do we ever think how important self-image is in how we think about ourselves - either as a victim or as an achiever? What we think of ourselves is what influences our lives.

Here is something to consider along this line. Being bad at something is the first step to becoming good at that something.

If you are good at something on the other hand it is hard work to get better. Does that make sense?

If we think we are dumb at math or couldn't ever figure out algebra while in school, we probably never would. If we put it in our mind that we were going to succeed in that supposedly weak area and did not let anything get in our way, no matter what or how long it took, it's almost a certainty that we'd achieve our goal and certainly get better.

Maybe this is a problem with those that consider themselves to be victims. Perhaps, it is their self-image that has made them the victim and not the circumstances of race, education, gender, or plain old bad luck. Think about it.

Speaking about victims and this seems to have taken a precedence in today's world especially here in the good old USA. So many think they are a product of victimization. But I say don't take it for what it really is. If you look up the definition it goes like this: A person who never takes responsibility for their lives.

There have been countless people that have been victims for some reason or another but have pulled themselves up by taking responsibility for their lives. What they found was that if we have determination and perseverance and put them into practice, others will give them a hand up and not just a handout.

What Comes Next?

The problem is a handout can lead to dependency and mediocrity, not responsibility. As the good umpire always says, I just call em like I see'em! This can lead to discussions. Discussions can be good especially if there is no name calling involved.

Give an example: Many years ago, I was told by my mentor that if I ever wanted to get ahead in the business world, I had to become a better public speaker.

While this shocked me at first, I took it to heart and after doing some research joined a local Toastmasters club. Took me a while but eventually I became a good public speaker. Probably not the likes of that famous orator of days past Willian Jennings Bryan but, good enough to become President, CEO and Chairman of the Board of the company at which I was employed, president of two Toastmaster clubs, Toastmaster of the Year, winner of a couple speech contests, president of two national trade associations.

Almost 40 years later I still value and continually work on improving my public speaking skills.

Believe me I still need to work on improvement.

What I'm getting at is if you are determined, are willing to apply yourself and persevere, no matter what others say, you can prove them wrong!

The secret is, change your ways. Instead of being afraid of change, welcome it. No one is ever too young or too old to change. Be careful of who you hang with. Negative people with negative opinions, especially of yourself, make all the difference.

Most of these types are either people we work with, people who are family members or our personal friends. Don't have much choice when it comes to people you work with but make sure you don't spend extra time with the negative thinkers.

Personal friends with negative attitudes are people we have a choice to avoid. Rosy attitudes make much better friends.

Now family is a whole other issue. Generally avoiding our family members with negative attitudes is a real problem. Just think of it this way, keep away from subjects where their negative comments will influence your decision making. That doesn't mean you still can't love them.

Here's another way to look at it by looking at you. Think about what is wrong with you. Example, instead of focusing on the negatives like am I too fat, too thin, too smart, too dumb, too good looking, too plain, remember that there are many other designations that can influence our self-image. A good way to think is, "What's right about us?"

Be honest and you will find a lot. After all God made no one else exactly like us. We may not be the best looking or whatever, but we have our attributes.

Now here is something that happened to me just yesterday. I was sitting in a salon waiting to get a haircut, two ladies were nearby talking. I heard one of them say, "I would vote for him just because he's so handsome."

I don't believe they were talking about me but, that was probably just fantasy not reality talking.

Well Adjusted

Self-image is not in my mind the goal of making you a superior, arrogant person. It is simply about making you see yourself as being the best you can possibly be. That is the most important way to see yourself. If you can do that others will see you in the same light.

How do you go about that? One way is to dream about seeing yourself as a well-adjusted individual.

What Comes Next?

Think about imagining being that well-adjusted person.

Ask yourself how a well-adjusted person reacts to both the good things as well as things or events that are not so good?

Good things are when people say nice things like, "Thank You" or you look good today, even, "Hey, want to go to lunch?"

This may be a comment from your boss, "Nice job, you handled that well."

If you are a golfer, it may be as simple as, "Nice shot!"

Of course, there are a lot more, but I think you get the point. Think about how a well-adjusted person would react.

Oh, if you are having problems adapting to well-adjusted, here is a suggestion. Go make an appointment with my son-in-law, Dr. Steve. He is a chiropractor, and he will make sure you are well adjusted. Just a suggestion!

Believe taking on the role of a well-adjusted person will solve many problems and make you feel better.

Now let's look at the other side and consider how our self-image reacts when we are scolded or we get a speeding ticket, have an accident that is our fault, or are screamed at by our spouse. Is it the end of the world? I think not.

Imagine how a well-adjusted person with a good self-image would handle the situation. Would they sulk, get defensive, scream back? Probably not, maybe not. I hope not.

Remember, if we scream back, act defensibly, etc., it will stay with us for a long, long time and help destroy the self-image and self-esteem we are trying to cultivate.

This is where our creative imagination comes into play. After all we are attempting to find and fertilize our best self.

Our chore then is to find and picture our best self, especially during stressful times. We don't have to be perfect, as nobody really is. It's what we must do if we are to change into this new role.

Use this technique and see how it works in the long run.

I know in my case it takes continuous work and is a never-ending process.

Again, use your creative imagination to picture how a well-adjusted person would act.

Consistency, determination, and practice are the means. Not easy but well worth the effort to find and help your best self flourish. Think about it.

Before I finish this topic, here is how I feel about the value of using your mental imaging to help with motivation. The point is we all need motivation. If we are not motivated, we will never accomplish anything of value. It's what I call positive association.

Again, it's our dreams that help us strive toward a goal. I suggest you review the section of this book concerning dreams and think about your dreams and how they have influenced your life in a positive manner. Then put together your dreams that are filled with goals.

Victimization / Entitlement Concept

Here is an area that seems to have creeped into our world today and that is the concept of entitlement or victimization.

Now, Entitlement is when a person thinks they have a "right." That right generally comes from those giving the entitled someone else's money or things. That may or not be true.

Victimization is more like a person who in the end does not take responsibility for their lives. This may seem harsh and heartless but just a fact of life.

For example, If I'm always a victim, whose fault is that? Probably with an angry attitude, it's our own fault.

What Comes Next?

After all, at some time or other we are all victims whether it be our fault or because of innocuous discrimination, medically, our looks or intellect, even events in our life. This can go on and on.

My point of view is never an entitlement or victim be! At least not for long.

Victimization can be hard to deal with and impact our entire life however, if we let it take control of our life the events or individuals that made us the victim we possibly never have a happy, fruitful life. That would be sad.

What is earned through your own efforts will be appreciated and valued a whole lot more. Much better to focus on the positive, eliminate the negative and don't mess with Mr. in between.

Get that anger out of our way and we will end up much happier. Oh, you can get mad once in a while, that's human nature. Even Jesus got mad when he kicked the pharisees out of the Temple.

I can remember many years ago when something bad happened in my life. At first, I couldn't understand why it happened and thought it was my fault, then I realized it was not.

It was what prompted me to get mad and take steps to get over it.

A few years later as an Executive Recruiter, I wrote an article for a division of the *Wall Street Journal* called, *Exit Statements vs Lame Excuses.*

It seems I got tired of potential clients coming into my office with great credentials on their resume, then crying to me for thirty or so minutes about their being down-sized, right-sized or whatever.

This article, published in the careers section of a division of *The Wall Street Journal,* was designed to help those who had lost their jobs or had something bad happen that caused their life to be disrupted. The focus was to empathize with people who got fired from their jobs, had a nasty divorce or even a physical calamity. The goal was to not spend a lot of worthless time making lame excuses for the event. Then next come up with an exit statement that describes in a true, clear, and concise manner what you learned from the experience and how what you learned will benefit the company with whom you are interviewing. This also works with friends and acquaintances.

The way I look at it I always prefer a refreshing story. Think we all do.

Mistakes

If you made a mistake, I emphasized don't be afraid to admit it and be able to explain how the experience will benefit you in the future. Trust me, we all make mistakes. We should learn from them. Lame excuses never helped a person get a new job or a lot of new friends. Likewise portraying one's self as a victim will never result in anything positive.

Here's another thought about the dangers of projecting the Superior Image described earlier regarding transforming our self-image and self-esteem to our true self.

We do not want to portray ourselves as being persons with a superiority image. Most experts believe that people who act this way have an inferiority complex and are really suffering from insecurity, thus this is a coverup.

Thinking back, I wish I had not yelled at others I respected. Even now on occasion I've mistakenly yelled at my wonderful wife and kids. That never worked out well. Guess I will have to keep working on reacting as a well-adjusted person like everyone else.

Being well adjusted is a great thing to be and that's fine. However, being well adjusted while you are under stress is a whole other animal. For example, have you ever been under stress and felt different?

Daily we all deal with stress of some sort. Especially right now during the pandemic. Note: hopefully by the time you read this most of the stress involved will have dissipated and we are on to something less dramatic. With stress we either adapt or we succumb.

It's what some call the wear and tear of living in today's dynamic world.

Many books have been written on the subject. Many by regular people, some by athletes and many by scientists. Don't think I'm qualified to prove any one of them. After all, I'm just a regular guy, not a trained expert on the subject.

My position is that the better we can handle our everyday stresses, whether it comes from work, play or even personal relationships, the better we will feel and act.

Stress

We all know people handle stress in a variety of ways.

Seems stress either helps us perform better or prevents us from doing our best.

Jerry West, Mr. Clutch of L.A. Lakers fame, and Joe Namath, football Hall of Famer, both claimed before each game, in the privacy of their locker room they would barf their guts out due to stress of performing their best. Others resort to the bottle to cover up stress wounds. Don't know how that works. Guess it depends on the extent. I will say I enjoy a libation but not as a stress solution.

Then there are those that depend on drugs. This has seemed to become more prevalent in recent years. There are mixed opinions on this as a stress solution. By the way, drugs are not my thing.

Many others pass off their stress issues to others. These may be their family members, spouse, or employees, even their so-called best friends. To me this is totally unfair and a bad solution.

As for a solution to the vagaries of stress, while I'm not a doctor or trained therapist on the subject, I have dealt with stress as all of us have and talked to many experts on this subject. Their solutions include many. For example, the story of Jerry West and Joe Namath. Just get over it and go about your business to be the best you can be.

Let's face it, some of us are more susceptible to stress than others. What I mean is that if you don't care there is no stress. Probably the greatest hero is the soldier, firefighter, police officer or other first responder that goes into danger scared out of their wits and reacts without regard to their personal safety. Don't you agree? After all, perhaps caring so much for others is underrated and is a real positive for the values of stress. Caring means a lot and certainly is instrumental in our self-image.

How important do we think self-image is? How does it impact our everyday life? Even more, do we ever think about it? Maybe it's time to....

How Do We Create a New Attitude to Enable Us to Make a Change?

This is a question that the experts have been asking for thousands of years. Even Jesus Christ, Son of God, had difficulty with this issue. I don't purport to be an expert, but I am the son of my mother and father and they always gave my sister and brothers simple advice: Follow your dreams and don't let others tell you otherwise. If I had enough time, I would give you examples of how this simple advice guided my sister and brothers in their lives. Let's go on from here.

Pulling Success from Failure

Our goal is to create a new attitude that takes us from a failure to success. Now this does not mean we have to go from being poor to instantly becoming wealthy. It is simply the result of pulling success (satisfaction) from failure, at least in our own mind. After all it's our mind that we are working on.

So, again I ask how do we change?

- How does a confirmed criminal become a model citizen?
- How does a shy person become a model of self-confidence?
- How do we take obsessions with our failures and turn them into success?

Here's something to consider: Denials foster our failures. Once we fail, then fail again, failure becomes a habit that can be hard to overcome.

However, while scars (failures) are hard to overcome, they can be overcome. Just think of inventor Thomas A. Edison. He did not let thousands of failures prevent him and his associates from inventing the lightbulb and movie projector along with many other marvelous life-changing devices. Then there was Alexander Graham Bell and the telephone.

What Comes Next?

Let's consider these scars as lessons learned. Like the old saying, "Don't do the same thing over and over and expect different results!"

In my mind the answer to turning from failure to success is consistency not instant self-gratification.

While most great sports figures, financial gurus, surgeons, inventors, etc. have natural talents, they did not fall into their success mode. Probably the most important key to their success is the consistency of working on their chosen field.

Here is a quote from Miyamoto Musoshi, the Japanese philosopher: "One thousand days of lessons for discipline, ten thousand days of lessons for mastery."

Tiger Woods, the best golfer of our time, claims the key to his proficiency was spending over 10,000 hours as a youth working on improving his golfing skills. Guess that worked out for him.

Then there is the renowned brain surgeon Dr. Ben Carson, who attributes much of his medical achievements to his dedication.

Here is a personal story (not me). It's about a young boy who was attacked by polio at an early age. The polio left him with a 90% disabled left arm, an arm he couldn't raise beyond his waist.

However, this did not stop him as he learned to overcome this disability.

His family loved to play golf, especially his father.

When he reached sixteen, his dad got him a job working in the golf shop of a local country club. Even with this disability, he learned and became a pretty darn good golfer. He played in high school and then later in college.

How did he do this? First it was simply his dream and he never let anyone tell him he couldn't. Next was his perseverance and determination. He always had those attributes in him, not only in becoming an aspiring golfer but in everything he did. At sixteen he took his driver's test, took him three tries but he got it. After graduating from college with an accounting degree, he was determined to get his CPA, which he did after having to take one of the parts a couple of times before succeeding.

Again, this shows the value of consistency, determination and not letting little failures or setbacks get in the way of his dreams.

Oh, and by the way he is now in his seventies and has been Club Champ at his Country Club eight of the last nine years. At the age of 73 he shot a 69. Oh heck, just learned today as I'm writing this that he just won his ninth championship in the last ten years. Still a rather good one-armed golfer, wouldn't you say? No self-gratification here. Likewise, no victim complex.

Do you know anyone who has overcome difficulties? If we think about it, probably we all do. Ask them:

- What happened that changed your life?
- What did you do about it?
- How did it turn out?

Here's another secret as I see it, get a self-image that you can live with, makes you happy and confident. It must be adequate, realistic and something you can believe in.

It must be reasonable. After all, we are not all Thomas A. Edison. By reasonable I mean you are neither more nor less than you are.

We want to utilize our capabilities to the fullest or as close as possible.

It must make you feel good. Make you feel self-confident. It also provides peace of mind, an important part of a successful, meaningful life, not only for you but for all those around you. I'm sure a successful, meaningful life is what we would like as our legacy.

Now you may wonder why I left "happy" out of what we want our legacy to be. Don't get me wrong. I value happiness as much as anyone. The only problem in my estimation of being happy is that it is different for each of us.

We are all happy in different ways. For some it's as simple as just having to do nothing to survive. For others, their happiness is giving to others. Then there are those who thrive on working on a meaningful project, being self-sufficient, being free to do as they choose as well as many other activities.

I'll bet you could ask just about anyone and each would give a different variety of what makes them "happy." Since there seem to be so many variables, let's substitute 'success' for happy. Meaningful also comes into play.

We can consider this as being our life instinct and we don't have to do it alone. That's why it is important to carefully pick who we hang with. Who do you think would make you a more self-confident person, one with a rosy helpful disposition or one that's constantly putting you down? Careful who you choose to influence your life.

Creative Imagination

This is my next issue. Think of it this way. Our mind is not a robot and I suggest it is more creative than any computer of this the electronic age. Now I'm not a computer guru but at least my brain doesn't crash two times per day. Well maybe.

How we use or don't use this God-given gift is up to us. Think about that for a moment. Then realize that we can learn to adjust, adapt, and thus overcome our failures, increase our happiness and success or whatever we strive for.

We are different than animals. Man has that creative imagination more than just instinct to survive and procreate as with animals. Again, this was provided by our own creator.

The human brain is amazing, but we've got to use it. This is what we will talk about next for a while.

Corrective Measures to Best Use Our Creative Imagination

This was hard for me to put together, but I hope it will make sense and I encourage you to come up with your own corrective measures that fit and will help to achieve creativity.

First, consider our sense organs. Think of it this way, our brain remembers success and forgets failures. For example, how do we suddenly remember a name we've temporarily forgotten? How do we remember taste, smell, even a voice not heard for years?

How do we suddenly relive a childhood memory forgotten many years ago?

This is a mystery of our amazing brain.

Consider this: we all make mistakes. However, mistakes don't make us, they help us learn. Without making mistakes, how would we learn what is right or wrong? How would we improve?

It's like happiness and sadness. Without sadness there would never be happiness. Sounds like something pathetic but, let me ask you, what would our lives be like to never have any happiness? Life wouldn't be all that rewarding. Think about that for a minute.

Here is another thought along that line. Often it is our imagination that leads to our misery. If we get over our own misery, we have a better chance that our attitude and confidence will change.

Get over it and don't let your miseries drag you down!

What Comes Next?

I've said this before but let's try it again, maybe we think others believe we look funny or that I'm dumb etc. Believe me, most people don't care what we look like or how smart we are. After all there will always be people that are both. This is just the misery of "only if" or of seeing ourselves in a negative manner.

Here's my suggestion, trust your creative imagination and do not be afraid of making mistakes. Consider the options and ask the question, "What's the worst that can happen?" Then take steps to ensure the worst doesn't happen. This takes trust.

Consider that without imagination we would never make improvements. The world would never improve, create new inventions, systems, or ways of doing things. We would still be below the level of the Stone Age.

Success is generally a result of trial and error. In fact, as I'm writing this, scientists across the world are using trial and error to find a vaccine to stop the pandemic. It's not just pure science that will do it but multiples of trials with many errors until they figure it out.

The key is to have a goal or target and to take the steps to reach what you are striving for.

Depending on how good you are at planning and implementing, the fewer mistakes you will make. I guarantee you the scientists looking for the vaccine are making many errors in their trials but, they are learning along the way. This is the way it works and do not wait until you have proof, otherwise it may never come to pass.

Your imagination is the first step to success.

Getting back to yourself, another key is to understand you. If we are to be as successful as we wish to be, there must be some justification. That is truth as you see it. This will help you imagine your new self-image and will contribute to how your new self-image ends up.

What Comes Next?

As a Master Gardener, I frequently give workshops to both experienced and inexperienced gardeners. It is not unusual to get comments from people that say I've got a "brown thumb" or "I kill everything I try to grow." I love to hear this because nobody has a "brown thumb." It's just that they don't know what they are doing.

Usually it takes me about 45 minutes to get them on the right track. Can't say how many times people have come up to me after having attended one of my workshops and said, "Thank you, your advice helped me grow a bountiful garden crop!"

I try to make something that seems mysterious or complicated SIMPLE.

For experienced gardeners accustomed to doing their gardening one way, it is more difficult. Generally, instead of 45 minutes it takes about three weeks. Oh well, it's nice when they come back and say WOW. Again, the mystery of change.

It's What We Do That Counts

We all think we know what a hero is. However, here is my interpretation. We don't all have to be heroes to do something others tell us it takes bravery to do. Heroic acts often are just a onetime thing with the hero being in the right place at the right time and doing the right thing. Others do heroic acts every day.

Those heroes are like soldiers in the military fighting battles every day. How about firefighters going into a burning building to save a stranded cat or a person or a baby or even just putting out a fire, without regard that they are doing a brave act that may put their life in danger.

However, bravery is not just when the bullets are flying. These acts are part of their job. Don't you think the spouse of a soldier or firefighter sending them off to do their daily duty, hoping they will return safely, is a hero? How about an employee going to their boss, at the risk of their job, to ask for a well-deserved raise?

Key point: Remember it's what we do that counts. I was told a long time ago your attitude and what you do with it is what people care about. Keep your attitude and imagination in the right track and you will see the difference.

Here are a few suggestions along this line:
- Do the right thing. Use this as your guideline.
- Think about others first. You will have a lot of allies.
- Help others. This will come back to you in spades. How can we expect others to help us when we are in need if we are not willing to help them?
- Let others see the good in you. You will never regret it
- Be a giver, not a taker.

Doing these things will help you see the truth in your imagination. Here are a couple of examples of the power of our imagination.
- Think you are cold, and you will be.
- Think you are hot, and you will be.
- This is true when you are hypnotized. Hypnotism is like magic and very surprising. When you think it's true while under hypnotism, it will be true to you at that time.
- Be your own hypnotist and use the magic to rid your imagination of its negativity.
- If you think it is true it will be...just like the person under hypnosis.

Our brain is an amazing thing. We react to what we think is true.

Human Nature

Don't you ever think that it is unusual for people to not do something when they are doing it?

It's like when you say you are not worried. You only say it when you really are.

Or when you say you don't care, but you really do?

These are excuses and are part of what is known as human nature. Usually this trait exposes itself when we are scared.

From what I surmise this is called by others the destructive instinct of humans. In other words, we probably all have it. The only thing is it probably is not what we can call normal human behavior. It is a defensive mechanism used by us humans, basically to justify or hide our actions.

In my opinion these are both good and bad actions, good in that it may help us for a moment or two, bad in that it is not the truth and we then are not being true to ourselves or others. As a result, our excuses can eventually come back to haunt us. Ugh.

The question then is if we want to work on self-improvement, that is probably furtive and almost impossible. Kind of like we were told as kids, one lie leads to many others, so don't lie, it's easier in the long run to simply tell the truth. This is especially true if it was an everyday part of our being and our lives.

Since this book is supposed to be a part of our dealing with change, self-esteem and self-image and eventually help us deal with what comes next. I guess we should be careful of what we say! Yes, human nature is a very mysterious thing. But, think about it, don't most of us want to improve every day?

Guess that was part of God's plan when we were given Free Will. We get to choose our actions.

What Comes Next?

If using a defensive mechanism to justify our being can be a bad part of human nature, do you ever do that? Don't feel bad, most of us do it sometime in our life. After all it is human nature and we are not perfect beings. Wish I knew how to overcome our bad instincts like this. All I can say is we can, but not alone. Remember that old saying, "No man is an island."

While we need good influences in our life, we also have something else. That is our creative imagination. Good influences can help us set our objectives and goals as well as achieve them. They can also benefit our demeanor.

Our creative imagination can be to exercise the power of being our own hypnotist. Spoke about this earlier. That is, if we imagine good in our minds, good will happen. Yes, we will believe it to be true.

If we work on it, have a good plan, be patient and consistent, this will enable us to successfully deal with changes and bad habits as they crop up. With that, we will see our self-esteem and self-image skyrocket.

Don't you think that the people we associate with can either have a positive or negative influence on us?

Again, it's not just how much money we can accumulate or how much money they have. Maybe they are our mom or dad, etc. or even our self-indulgence. Oh, and don't forget we can also influence others with our behavior.

My suggestion is to use that amazing brain to help solve problems or issues. Oh yeah, that creative imagination, especially with the help of others like a mentor, pastor, minister, priest, rabbi, or a capable friend.

By the way, in the process of writing this book I asked for comments from people I trust. Amazing what I heard back, things such as I like your stories, or even how about with the stories, more of your personal input.

P.S., I don't know why they would want more of my personal input, but I will try.

Believe me, it's difficult to write a book of this nature. Couldn't do it without the help of others like Editor Lee Pound. Often, I get probed with questions like, "What did you mean by that?" Or maybe, that phrase is inappropriate or let's put it another way.

Oh well, they say the life of a writer is very lonely, and I can agree with that especially with the pandemic in full force. Thank God the golf courses are now open where we live and at least I can go out to the driving range, maintain my social distance, and beat some golf balls when at a mind block stage. Does it work? Mostly yes.

By the way I use this method also when doing crossword puzzles. Let the puzzle set for a while when I get stuck. Pick it back up later and voila! the answer is right there. At least most of the time.

Perhaps it can be worth it if you can get your story out. Even more so if your story influences others in a positive manner.

Lee Pound has always said, "Everyone has a story, not everyone tells their story." Thanks, Lee for helping me get my stories out.

Intestinal Fortitude

What does that mean? According to Webster's, it's simply guts, courage or bravery, perseverance or grit. Don't know how brave we must be but believe we all have perseverance that enables us to get up every day to go to work or get done what needs to get done. Most of the time that can take guts, grit or what is known as intestinal fortitude. Think of it this way, don't you think it takes grit to go to work for fifty years through the good and the bad?

Why am I talking about this? Well here goes, where do you think we get that commodity called intestinal fortitude?

In my opinion it boils down to desire and instinct. Without these qualities how would we deal with every day?

Likewise, this is what makes the difference in people. Contrary to what politicians tell us, it's not race, gender, net worth, or education, it's our brain and how we use it. This is what makes the difference between us and animals.

Imagine yourself being successful. Chances are your self-confidence and self-image will improve dramatically. It will certainly improve your skills, happiness, and success.

As an Executive Recruiter I used to suggest that a person preparing a resume start by making a list of their skills. This will help qualify them for the position. Next make a list of things they have done in their career that they were most proud of. These were things that either made money, saved money, or saved time for the company.

To do this, start from the most recent and go backward. This method would enable them to think backward and remember the things from years they had forgotten. The key was to just start writing and not quantify. They could do that later.

By using this method, they could prep themselves and raise their level of confidence during an interview, especially when asked by an interviewer, "Why should I hire you?"

In other words, it becomes the differentiator between their competitors. Usually we don't think about the things we would have liked to tell the interviewer until we are driving home. Too late.

What Comes Next?

This system would give them a real advantage over their competition as while most would say I'm loyal, dedicated, eat my lunch at my desk, never take time off. All BS answers.

My candidate could say, "Here's what I've done that made money, saved money, or saved time. How can I help you?"

It would also raise your level of self-confidence.

You can get more info and details by going to Amazon books, enter Mark Fierle in the search bar, and consider buying my book *Rekindling the American Dream*. Believe you will like it based on its reviews. It's available in both e-book and soft cover formats. It has a five-star classification.

OK, back to intestinal fortitude. Try role playing to picture your success with the help of your imagination.

Your physical brain and body functions as a machine that you operate. Use your brain to imagine what you want to accomplish. You must have a goal to achieve. Then set your goal and imagine how you will accomplish this.

Again, it must be realistic, achievable and have a time frame. Without that it's a fantasy. Also keep in mind most people coast, never thinking what they really want or what it will take to achieve. They don't want to rock the boat.

My suggestion: Be ready to accept the bad with the good as there will always be some of each.

Be sure to follow what I discussed earlier and work on your attitude all the time.

Now if you are like most of the modern generation, you are used to instant gratification. However, as depicted earlier it took Tiger Woods over 10,000 hours of diligent work to become probably the greatest golfer of his era, maybe ever. His key was first ability and second consistency.

For change to happen we must remember the laws of change.

This is not written down like the Bible, but it still applies. Do not consider that we want to make a change. It will just happen and stay with us. I've heard that it takes time and consistent implementation to make a significant adjustment.

Then you need to work on it. Perfectly.

Practice Makes Perfect

You've heard the old saying, "Practice makes perfect." That may be true up to a point. I like to think that perfect practice has a better chance of success than imperfect practice. What do you think?

The key then is do not think about instant results, that almost never happens with good results. Instead think about constant implementation of the change you want to occur. Some say that change can take a long time, maybe three weeks, maybe years. If you can change from a negative attitude to a success, it will all be worth it. With that attitude, *What Comes Next* won't be so overwhelming.

I Wonder

I Wonder, a few observations… then we will get back to self-image and self-esteem.

I wonder what it would be like for Americans to trust again. Maybe being honest would help, this includes the politicians in our government. Don't think we've seen much of that lately.

What Comes Next?

I wonder what it would be like to be able to trust our fellow man, regardless of their race, religious convictions, creed, age, or social standing. Trust but verify was a mantra during the Reagan administration. However, that was aimed at Russia, not our fellow citizens and government. Hope we can all work on that.

I wonder what it would be like to have objective journalism again in America. Last time I checked a real journalist did not have an agenda. Their worth was proven by probing for the truth based on facts and research. This was called investigative journalism and was backed up by at least three reliable sources. It wasn't just that the journalist or their medias opposed the subject. If it were, this would then be called opinion.

Will Rogers, the noted humorist and philosopher who died in a plane crash in the 30's, used to say, "The only things I know are what I read in the newspapers." Today it seems we have a difficult time trusting the media on almost anything. A shame!

I wonder if we can work on uniting us as Americans rather than saying "I'm a uniter," then immediately go about dividing one race against another or rich vs. poor etc. One thing I learned playing golf, we are all equal on the golf course. Would be nice to be able to think our fellow citizens are equal based on what they do.

I wonder what it would be like to protest or celebrate without creating a riot? Damaging other people's property is still a sin even when not prosecuted as a crime. Maybe we should prosecute rioters that destroy property. What do you think?

I wonder what it would be like to walk downtown day or night and not be accosted or called a bad word if you gave a handout less than the accoster felt they deserved? Is this the

What Comes Next?

result of the entitlement society that has sprung up in recent years? I know this phenomenon is the same in almost every city of some size. Recently my wife and I were accosted six times after leaving a Los Angeles Kings hockey game just walking back to the parking garage. Probably would have been cheaper and safer to hire a bodyguard. I asked a local cop if that was normal? He said it was even worse. How sad!

I wonder what it would be like to get a higher education without having to adhere to a professor's biased political agenda. How many students are faced with this dilemma, especially while attending major universities? It's either adhere or be castigated. Doesn't sound like education to me, more like brainwashing.

I wonder what it would be like rather than being considered aggressors against certain sections of our population, police were given the respect they deserve instead of defiance. It is sad to hear about the disrespect these first line responders are faced with, even just trying to buy a cup of coffee.

Same goes for our military, firefighters, even teachers. This probably started during the 1960's but has grown exponentially since 2008. Where did this come from? As Aretha said, how about some R-E-S-P-E-C-T.

I wonder what it would be like again to respect marriage as a sacred union between a man and a woman? Likewise, respect given to all unions without trying to call it something that it is not. Even President Lincoln said you cannot call a tail on a dog a fifth leg! A tail is a tail, not a leg. A marriage is between a man and a woman. Let our eternal creator be the judge.

What Comes Next?

I wonder what it would be like for there to be a men's bathroom and a woman's bathroom. Since when do transgenders or others whose behavior is considered abnormal get to use whatever facilities they choose. Guess it comes down to plumbing!

I wonder what it would be like to not consider social media as the gold standard. After all, since Google, Facebook, and Twitter are supposed to know everything, do they really have to, or do we want them to?

I wonder what it would it be like for people to express different opinions without denigrating their opponents by offering slurs on their character, calling them bigots or other bad names? That is a weak and meaningless excuse for not having a real response. I always thought that having a meaningful dialog usually leads to mutual resolution. At least with somewhat intelligent people.

Oh, and I wonder what it would be like to play an evening nine holes of golf, walk and carry my golf bag and it would only cost $5.00? Guess I will have to go back thirty years. Note: had to throw that in for just a bit of levity. Times have changed. Will I get over it? Maybe not.

Part II

Story Updates

Updates of Stories

Traditionally in my books I have included some stories of people who have been successful, then have gone through difficult times and have the intestinal fortitude to overcome and prosper. Thought I would include a few of them in this issue along with updates of how they are doing now. From there we will go back to the subject of change, self-image, and self-esteem.

Our first story is about a guy named Robert Pedregon. The story is called *First Night Out.* and goes back a few years. It's the story of a man who followed his dreams.

Joseph Wambaugh, Michael Connelly, ad infinitum, have told the story of policemen and their experiences in the world of law enforcement.

Millions of police novels have been sold and countless TV series have invaded our screens with their tales of the lower edge of life. Some remember the short run TV series *The Rookies,* stories of young cops. Most of the stories weave around experienced detectives that have an altered perspective of life with broken marriages, booze, drug and anger problems; a sad perspective on life based on their dealings with upholding the law and protecting citizens from cold-blooded murderers and the underside of society as a whole. With all the negatives and dangers involved, we wonder why anyone with a normal upbringing would consider entering a law enforcement career. After all, one of the major reasons police officers leave the career they have chosen is mental stress leading to early retirement. A man can only take so much. Maybe it's something about doing the right thing!

My story today will involve three young men with idealistic motives and a desire to do the right thing and have a great career in law enforcement. I hope after reading this you will get an idea of what they faced and why they do it.

November 6, 2009 was a beautiful sunny and warm fall day in Los Angeles. We drove up to the L.A. Police Academy for graduation of the 509 Class. This is the culmination of over six months training for the 44 remaining graduates of a starting class of 71. They even had one candidate fail after the badge ceremony just 30 days ago. The falloff was huge.

The standards are high. Some will have the opportunity to join a later class and go through the entire process again; others will not have the opportunity. Emotions are high and we are particularly proud of our new cop. He is not like the others. First, he is 43 years of age while most of the class is 22 or 23 years of age, and fresh out of the military.

In other words, buff and in shape and accustomed to the military-type discipline of the Academy. Training ranges from intense Marine Boot Camp physical training every day to mental torture learning the statutes of the law that guide police work and being questioned unerringly about why you can be so stupid as to give an answer like that! Haven't you been paying attention? Humiliation is a daily occurrence. After all, you can't be a cop without knowing the law and how it is interpreted in the eyes of our politically correct judicial system.

For example, if you can provoke a cop with your actions and he/she is compelled to lay a hand on you, he will have been deemed justified in putting your lights out, not just slapping you away.

The consequences are the same. You go before a commission and it sounds like either you slapped him because you felt you were in danger or you knocked his lights out because you were in danger. Which seems more logical? The law and the longevity of a law enforcement officer is dependent on interpretation and acting on it based on procedure, training, and good judgment.

Our cop trainee had gone through a life up to this point where he drove a long-haul truck for years in support of his family's transport business. He learned a lot during this period, especially how to meet schedules and overcome obstacles of the road. He had saved his money during this time and after getting married and having a child, he opened a retail coffee shop.

At one point, he owned several, along with a pizza parlor.

Things were going well until one day he woke up and realized his marriage was over. The adage of when one door closes another one opens came into play here. In this case he met a young girl that became the love of his life, Nicole. Then after 10 years of building his business into a successful enterprise, his world came crashing down again. Six months before his lease was up for renewal, his landlord informed him they would not be renewing...a Starbucks wanted the property. Now, what to do?

Of course, this was not going to stop him. He was determined to make the best of it.

Something he always wanted to do was to become a police officer. He began applying to local police departments. Although most were in a hiring freeze due to the economy. He also went into a physical regime that resulted in his being in the best physical shape ever. He would need it.

What Comes Next?

Finally, he was accepted into the California Highway Patrol, not as an officer, but as a 911 Dispatcher, his hope being that eventually he would get to wear a uniform. He went through training and in Sacramento was awarded the number one graduate award and was even offered the opportunity to move to Sacramento to be part of the Governor's Elite Guard, a great honor and opportunity. He turned it down as his son was here in Southern California and he did not want to leave him. Austin is his pride and joy.

Returning to his 911 Dispatcher job, he excelled and a few months later one of his applications came through. He was accepted into the next class of the Los Angeles Police Academy for the Los Angeles World Police, the Agency that covers the L.A. Airport and surrounding area. The class commenced in May 2009. To the recruits, being transformed from a civilian to a trained and ready uniformed cop is the beginning of hell. The lucky graduates are considered the "best of the best." There were three in his class designated for the LA World Police. Two made it, including him.

Opening day in the academy was easy. The next six months were not. It started with intense physical training. Long runs, calisthenics, learning techniques, self-defense, handcuffing, take downs, and academics.

Because of his age, he was made a show of the class, that is, if he scored better than a younger candidate, they were told, "How can an old man like that beat you out?"

This did not set well with his competitors as he generally did beat them out, including in the most rugged events. Even his DI called him "Old Man." Finally, one day, after excelling, the DI started calling him by his last name, "Pedregon." He felt like he got a promotion! His fellow candidates began to respect him as they realized what he was accomplishing and what kind of guy he was.

What Comes Next?

Along the way, he and two of his fellow candidates joined up into a study and technique training group. Each weekend they would work out and study together. This was a seven-day-per-week endeavor for the team of three, Rob, Bret, and Joe.

Eventually they made it through all the experiences of the academy like being "tasered" and "gassed." We got to see videos of these and believe me you would not want them to happen to you. In October they got their Badges but still had 30 days to go until graduation. These were critical days as five months had passed and if you failed now it would not have been worth it.

Coming down to the end, they faced critical tests of self-defense, types of shooting, day and nighttime work, and evaluation of skills. So far so good, except for one self-defense event where Rob let up a bit on one of his mates and he had to do a retest. Not making it meant no graduation. But he made it fine.

Then 10 days before graduation, Rob tweaked his hamstring. This was the day before they were to do a 4.5-mile run up Suicide Hill, a killer on a good day but excruciating with a bad leg. They told him he could skip it but would not be able to graduate until the next class. This was not acceptable.

He not only finished the routine that day, but made Suicide Hill the next day, a Friday (note: a bit slower than he would have liked). That weekend he was in miserable pain, but he was looking forward to the traditional Monday "Pride" run from the academy to the beach in Santa Monica. There was no way he was going to miss it. Running into the ocean that Monday just as it was called, A Thing of Pride! Now it is time for graduation and Rob, Bret, and Joe all made it. Both Bret and Joe told me at the graduation that it was the determination and help of Rob that inspired them along the way. I know that Rob feels the same about them. They are all three GREAT GUYs and will be a pride to the force.

What Comes Next?

Oh, by the way, Joe was honored at the graduation and got to carry the Academy Colors during graduation. Rob had the honor of carrying the Star-Spangled Banner in the Color Guard. It was spectacular and emotional.

Rob was also recognized by the Chief with a top academic honor and missed the top overall graduate by 1-8th of a point. That darn tweaked leg muscle before the Suicide Hill Run!

Now the guys had their assignments. Rob, of course, had two weeks more training at the Airport, Joe got Hollenbeck- the land of drugs and gangs, and Bret got Hollywood, the land of homeless and bums.

First Night Out

Now comes part two of the story, Joe's first night out. He and his training partners are called out late that night on a gang/drug bust. They and several other cops in their squadron break down the door on a gang house. The minute that happens, all hell breaks loose in the house and the perp occupants all scattered. One guy gets out and heads for the bushes. Joe is called to take off after him, finally corralling the guy and handcuffing him. Joe told Rob that he had never been so scared in all his life. Afterall, he didn't know if the guy had a gun or a knife or other cohorts in the homeboy neighborhood. Everything turned out ok but what a First Night Out!

Bret experienced something similar working in Hollywood a few nights later. Most of his action had been routine with their share of homeless, minor burglaries, and drunks to bust.

However, one evening he and his partner were cruising down the boulevard when suddenly, they heard a ping. Someone had shot a bullet through their squad car's windshield. Fortunately, no one was hit, but ladies and gentlemen, it's dangerous out there.

Rob had several interesting events in his first few weeks. His training officer/partner had a name for all his trainees. For Rob it is "The Scorpion." Seems his shaved head reminded him of "you guessed it." Then one evening he was doing crowd control as Brittney Spears was returning from an overseas event and was caught on camera by the TMZ Channel shoving a paparazzi out of the way. His training officer gave him some hell over this as he said, "We are not an escort service." Oh well, live and learn.

A few days later they took a guy that had been exiled from England into custody. As he was a US Citizen, they had to take him to Van Nuys for indoctrination. Along the way, he complained to Rob's training officer demanding to know the whereabouts of the three million dollars he brought with him. The training officer asked Rob if the guy had three million dollars. Rob said, "Yes sir he did, in Monopoly!" There are all kinds. Another incident a few days later was the arrest of two women with two hundred pounds of cocaine in their luggage going from LA to NY. Just routine, but it was a big deal on the LA news for a few days. There are a lot of stories out there. These are just a few in the early careers of three officers out of the Academy.

It also shows what perseverance, determination, and following your dreams can bring you. Not easy, but when is anything good not worth working for?

You can see I am proud of this man and his fellow compatriots who risk their life to keep us safe every day. Not only that but they had the gumption to follow their dream!

Hope you can use this as a beneficial example to follow your personal dream path. My father used to say that if you do something you really love, you will never have to work a day in your life.

Don't know if I followed that advice my entire career, but I'm doing it now.

A few years later he is an experienced officer and has been promoted three times. And is now a "111," a member of the prestigious LAPD honor Guard, a Distinguished Expert Marksman (Note: there are very few), and has been used as a "model" on World Police Recruiting promotions., entered and passed the Motor Academy. He is now a Motor Cop at LAX, has a high arrest and conviction record and has received the highest award given in the State of California the "Governor's Medal of Valor" Award. This medal was given for going above the Call of Duty in an event at LAX. Likewise, he was awarded the Medal of Valor Award by the California Peace Officers Association.

Here's the story and how I understand it went down.

November 1, 2013 was a beautiful day morning in Los Angeles. LA is a thing of beauty on days like this.

Only problem, evil people can turn beauty into ugliness and destroy other's lives, hopes, and dreams just with one evil act.

Our hero Rob was on morning shift in his patrol car on Century Blvd. not far from the airport. Then came the call "shooting at terminal 3." No other knowledge available.

With that he spun his car around and raced to terminal 3. Within 38 seconds he exited and ran into the terminal entrance, still with no information available, only a bunch of passengers panicking and getting out. By then a few more Officers arrived. Without having much info to go on, the team assembled. Fortunately they had trained the prior two weeks on such a happening.

What Comes Next?

The lead sergeant, Rob and three other Officers took pursuit. Passengers were fleeing one way, they went the other. Their pattern was a diamond formation with one in front (the lead) one in back to cover their rear and one on each side to cover their flanks. Rob was on the right wing.

They found a dead TSA agent, a wounded passenger, and a mostly deserted terminal. Note: later they found a few hiders.

Still they had little info on how many shooters were involved or where they were. Only info coming in was from panicked passenger cell phones. They did know shots were coming from an automatic high-powered rifle. They were outgunned, not a good thing as they only had their Glocks.

They proceeded according to department tactics without regard to their own safety. Hearing activity, they forged ahead. Then the first shots came at them.

Winston Churchill once said nothing is more exhilarating than having shots fired at you... and missing.

Now at least they knew where one of the shooters was and none of them had been hit yet even though the shooter was firing on auto and many of the bullets were near misses. Later the FBI told Rob one of the shooter's bullets missed his right temple by less than an inch. Now it's time to take him down.

And here is where the police training comes into play. Under the plan the lead sergeant would take the first shots with Rob alertly at his right flank.

With exposure the sergeant executed it to perfection and took him down.

On command and without regard to his personnel safety Rob raced forward and kicked the gun from the killer's arm. Assessing the damage calmly he faced the shooter eye to eye. He had secured the scene and saw that the man was bleeding out. They couldn't do much as they still didn't know if other shooters were out there but, as good officers they did their duty and saved the dirty, rotten, evil SOB.

Now as all the excitement is over, all this happened within a space of less than 4 minutes, 38 seconds for Rob to reach the scene and 3 minutes to gather the squad , make a plan and execute it to perfection.

Training, presence, confidence in the team and system saved many lives that fateful day. It was revealed the scumbag shooter had a note reading "Kill TSA and the PIGS!" I have met his teammates and had some nice conversations with the lead sergeant. He told me how proud he was to have Rob at his side that day. He couldn't stop issuing his praise of how Rob acted under the highest of pressure and would be honored to have him at his 6 (back) under any circumstances. This from a man that served in combat in the military as well as a gang sergeant with LAPD where he had experience in gunfights.

I asked him how he was coping with the shooting. He told me he was having some problems. I told him he and his team are in my prayers every day.

Thank God for these brave men that risk their lives every day to save our sorry souls.

So that's our update on Police Officer 111 Motors Unit Los Angeles World Police, Robert Pedregon. I asked my daughter Nicole how he handles what he does every day. She said, "He chose a life of service."

Shortly after the Chief asked him to take over as Public Information Officer (PIO). What an honor.

That's not all, October 2015, Chicago, Ill. Secretary General of InterPort Police and Chair of 9/11 Award Committee on terrorism has awarded Officer Robert Pedregon the 2015 Medal of Heroism and Valor! My gosh, I guess I will have to be more respectful to my son in law!

What Comes Next?

Rob followed his dream of being a serving Police Officer and has brought honor to his family, friends, his team and fellow officers, the city on and on.

In the military they say when pinning a medal on a soldier for bravery "He stood up and was counted." INDEED. This Blue doesn't run.

This is not easy, hardly ever is but, if we are to succeed consider Rob's example and follow your dreams.

What has happened during the years serving as PIO at LAX where every news event involving the Airport would go through him. Frequently we would get calls from all over the country saying, "Just saw Rob on TV."

It was an eventful time as he was on call 24-7. Don't think we ever had a family dinner that wasn't interrupted by calls from local or national media reporters. Along the way he got to meet two presidents, Obama and Trump, when they flew into LAX.

But Rob had his dreams and in early 2020 he applied for testing as sergeant. Among around thirty applicants from the force he was one of three to get the slot. This was no small feat as these several slots only come up every few years as approved by the LA city Council. He has completed his sergeant training and is now back on the street at the Airport. We pray for his safety every day.

By the way, his Badge still shines.

The Doc and The Girl Update

This is another epic story about two young people just out of school. He had just got his Doctorate in chiropractic medicine and she, her master's in film production.

What Comes Next?

Only problem, with the recession in full bloom unless you had an established clientele practice there was no place for a new Doctor. You may recall from my *Rekindling the American Dream* book he could only find work two days per week in the Chiropractic field and had to work as a "handyman" the rest of the time.

She on the other hand had a different problem, they were no longer making films in Los Angeles. She took a low-level job at Paramount Studios and fortunately got three promotions in two years. It was a good experience as she got to work on a few high-profile TV shows like *Dr Phil*, *American Idol* and *Dancing with the Stars*.

However, this was not either of their dream jobs. The Doc made some inquiries and found a practice in Columbia SC where he could manage one of the Doctor owner's practices. His goal was to learn the everyday operations of a practice and eventually open his own practice. They moved to Columbia, SC.

She quit her job at PARAMOUNT and moved without a job. With some diligent networking that did not last long she got a position at the Fox TV station in Columbia. They had her do several creative things during that initial time including special reports. She was told by her boss, "We'll probably learn more from you that you will learn from us!"

This was just the beginning and again as with PARAMOUNT she had several promotions and was eventually promoted and received "the leadership" award among a group of manager types at the Columbia Dale Carnegie Leadership class. With another promotion she began working with the sales staff handling large clients that wanted more for their advertising dollars. With this she was responsible for over one million dollars annually of station revenue. Big deal for a person with no training in sales.

What Comes Next?

With her help I was able to write a few chapters in my book *Unbridling the American Spirit*.

I mentioned that the DOC wanted his own practice. Unfortunately, that wasn't possible in Columbia and through some diligent research The Doc found a practice in Austin, Texas that seemed to be a good fit. He made an offer, it was accepted so they moved once again. Without a job, the girl did her research and had three job offers in Austin before they moved.

One was with CBS, another with a company outside the media world and another with the FOX TV channel. She accepted the FOX offer as it was a broadening of her horizons. The title was Executive Assistant to the General Manager of the station.

The station was the first TV station in Austin originally founded and owned by Ladybird Johnson, wife of President LBJ. In fact, her office was Ladybird's office.

Her responsibilities included solving every problem that came up at the station. She loved it and while learning a lot, the next year she was awarded "Unsung Hero" by the women's media in Austin. A big honor to say the least.

Oh, and by the way she just got a big important promotion as program director of the station.

So how is the Doc's new practice going? While it started out a bit slow, the Doc did his networking and each year it has become better and better.

In summary while they started out with a bad situation through diligence, perseverance, and determination they are well on their way. So proud of them.

Greg Edwards Update

Here is the update on another rags to riches and back to rags and again back. It is the story of Greg Edwards…

You may recall Greg from my *Rekindling the American Dream* book as well as the last update in my *Unbridling the American Dream* book. Here is where Greg has landed since we last spoke about his new company.

This is in Greg's own words: It has been 16 years since my first company ended in bankruptcy.

At the time, it was devastating.

I had spent 11 years building a company that when started had great promise embroidering logos on shirts for distributors and major companies around the country. Looking back on it--it was a less than perfect business model. No idea what revenue you would have in two months at the mercy of the economy {What company is ordering golf shirts after 911 or in 2008??), high fixed overhead (machines, rent, and skilled workers), and to top it off...you are sewing logos on $20.00 shirts...one slight machine mistake and you can wreck 15 of them in a few seconds.

After trying my hand at entrepreneurship, I ended with zero dollars in the bank.

It was time to take a step back and provide my young family with some steady income. Joined a large company, the Compass Group, and began an eight-year journey selling services to hospitals. I really enjoyed the work and learned a ton. The most important lesson of all--is what is called Recurring Revenue. I quickly realized what a beautiful revenue model The Compass Group had. You win a contract for cleaning, maintenance, internal patient transport, food, or laundry...And it never ends.

What Comes Next?

They will always need that service, and your team, if they are good, becomes part of the hospital community, part of the family. Why would the hospital ever switch? You must not be motivated to grow with them-for them to cancel your contract. Every month--the same recurring revenue--month after month. Compared to my embroidery business--it was 100 times better of a business model. And the niche of healthcare--never really goes through major ups and downs. (I'm writing this during the pandemic-so not "never" --but for many healthcare companies -- it has created opportunities).

Along comes my high school friend (a high net worth wall street guy) and he says, "Want to buy a business together?"

I said, "Sure! What are you buying?"

His answer, "I do not know...figure it out!"

Oh boy! I thought he had some struggling company he was going to buy for a song, and I would run it.

So, I was on a quest to figure out what service, in healthcare, could I get involved in. Was there a company that was in that space--that we could buy them? Way harder than I thought it would be. Long story short -- I landed on valet parking vehicles at hospitals. I had always noticed that many of the hospitals I visited had parking problems. More patients, visitors, and guests than the facility was designed for. And it met my criteria: Healthcare, recurring revenue, and if you are good, you just keep adding locations while losing very few.

We ended up not buying a company, but instead giving away a portion of the equity to a company in the healthcare valet space. They taught me all about the business, allowed me to use their references (for a few years we used their company name as our name). It took nine months to get our first account (which we still have today) but we took off from there. Six years later, the company has 75+ locations and over 10 million in revenue.

What Comes Next?

Those were just a few updates of people that I highlighted in both my *Rekindling the American Dream* and *Unbridling the American Spirit* books. These profiles show the locations and over $10 million in revenue. The most exciting part is that earlier this year, I was able to buyout my partner/friend and pay off the equity to the company that helped us get started –so I am now 100% owner. It has been a heck of a journey, had lots of fun along the way and am excited about the next chapter of growth and eventual sale of the company.

My biggest learning has been: If you're going to put your heart and soul into a business, think long and hard about the business model first, then find something you love after that, and build the spirit that enables each of them to do well, have a difficult time and come back strong.

See, we all have difficult times. Life is just not a straight line. However, having followed the three scenarios for the past ten years has been inspiring. I'm so happy to share these stories with you and I hope they have inspired you as well.

By the way just learned that Greg's company has been recognized by the State of Tennessee as one of it's the top four fastest growing companies. Congratulations, Greg!

Part III

Creating a Positive Attitude

Self-Image

This chapter will spend some time on self-image and will deal with a few of the issues that often hold back people like us, and a few ideas on how we can overcome.

First let's discuss Rejection.

Rejection or fear of rejection often holds people back a good part of their lives. It often prevents a person from doing the things that create acceptance or maybe full satisfaction.

Think of it this way, it has been said 90% of success is just showing up! If that be the case, why don't we just show up? We then have a better chance of not being rejected. On the other hand, many feel that if they don't show up, they will never fail. It's like if you don't try you will never be accused of missing.

The question is why don't we just show up all the time? Simple answer, the fear of rejection.

At some point in life we seem to all be impacted by that affliction.

Now here is another part of that malady, Successful salespeople talk about the number of No's or rejections it takes to get a Yes. Most say, especially for new salespeople, that it takes at least ten No's to get one Yes.

Now, this is a general statement and maybe that's ok for rookies, but veterans are also impacted with rejections to some point. Depends on a lot of things, including what you are selling, how you are going about the task, who you are presenting to, even what day of the month it is and are you asking for the order?

What Comes Next?

Of course, there are many other factors. However, most successful salespeople agree that a key is asking for the order. So when should that be done? I was told early on- ALL THE TIME. Now, some of us are bolder than others and they generally ask more frequently. Why don't us that are less bold ask more frequently?

Again simply, our self-image may not be strong enough to accept even one Rejection. That's too bad. Miss out on a lot of easy yeses that way.

We don't have to be selling a given product. Here's an example from my own personal experience. I remember going to high school in the city while I lived out in the "country." I always thought that's how the city kids thought of me, especially the girls, as a bumpkin and maybe I was to some degree.

One Friday night I gathered up the courage to go to the Friday Sock hop at the school gym.

Remember those?

All night I stood on the sideline talking to the guys attempting to build up my courage to ask this girl standing along the sidelines if she would like to dance?

However, I just stood there afraid to ask her in case she said "no thanks" or laughed in my face. Again, the fear of rejection.

Oh, to be 14 again.

I wondered for a long time after, what would have happened if I took the chance and asked her?

Guess we will never know. That's the way it is, we will never know.

The moral being ASK and you will find out, may even be pleasantly surprised. The same goes when you are trying to sell something, maybe to the girl at a dance, your boss, wife, the used car salesman or whoever, ask for the order often... Surprise yourself.

What Comes Next?

Rejection doesn't have to be all that injurious to your self-esteem, ego, or self-image.

Remember what I said earlier a good ratio in sales is 1 yes to 10 no's or rejections. Another way to look at it is, the more rejections you get the closer you are to a yes! Improve those odds by being smarter. That is, learn from your mistakes. This is what many successful people do: they try things, make mistakes, and learn from them. Remember Edison and other top achievers. Not to say you have to make mistakes, just be smart about it and use your amazing brain. As for me, thank the good lord I was a quick learner, took the advice of the good people I hung around with or at least tried to associate with.

Basically, they advised to use the experience you have gathered as well as that of others and figure out how it will better work. Next, we will get into a feature that only you have, and it is unlike anyone else. It is a unique feature of your amazing brain.

Imagination and Dreams

Imagination along with our brain are two of the things that make us unique as individuals. How we use both are up to us. For both to be as effective as can be requires a great deal of work.

For those of us that are lazy (and aren't we all to an extent) our God given gift goes to waste.

In this section I will address utilizing our imagination. I won't try to overemphasize or create something new as I don't believe my brain to be overly endowed but, at least think I have a good imagination that helps me use my brain at least occasionally.

Don't also know if everyone that knows me necessarily agrees and I promise to do my best. You can be the judge.

What Comes Next?

My first consideration is a part of our imagination that involves our Dreams. To me dreams have a part in our being. However, you have to be careful with them. They can be at times like a nice cold glass of water in the desert... Only problem, you can't drink it!

A real dream must be somewhat realistic, achievable within our ability to come true with time and hard work.

This is what I call our "strategy." We can all have achievable dreams and one of the hard parts is to create the "tactics" that will eventually enable us to make our dreams come through. Because most of us don't put in this hard work we may have a lot of dreams, but they never come true. Then we stop dreaming, especially as we get older.

Just a quick question or two: what are your dreams? Do you have any? What are your tactics to see them come true? If a dream you had came true, was it plain old luck or are the one's you've had merely a fantasy?

Young people seem to me to have many more dreams than older folks. Most of these are fantasies, others are nightmares. Older people who think their dreams never come true stop having fantasies, just have nightmares.

Now here is my suggestion: when you have a dream that you would really like to come true, develop your tactics that will help along that line. Start small and create four or five objectives that will get you closer to your dream. Then develop the tactics that will enable your dream to come truer.

The more you do the closer you will get. If it's just a fantasy, forget about it.

Example: if you always wanted a dream vacation house up in the mountains or down at the beach put together a plan, pick a location, develop a savings plan, etc. Sounds simple, huh? After a time, you can review and evaluate your plan and its progress. By reviewing your plan, you can see what's working and what needs to be altered. Oh, remember that guy from India that I mentioned at the beginning of this book, what do you think he had, a plan or a fantasy?

Dreams are generally good although nightmares are not. Fantasies are just that. I know my wife dreams often, probably every night. Generally, it is about her mom or dad and something they did in her life with them. Often, it's about her kids and someplace or time in their life. She even dreams about doing things with her besties. Seldom does she know if that's good or bad. On the other hand, she believes she has special powers and her dreams are true. Don't know about that. I know she is not a "witch" probably more like a guardian angel.

Enough about dreams. Hope you are still dreaming, and they are not all fantasies or nightmares. Dreams in my opinion (no real scientific research) are good for us, they stimulate our brain and imagination. I've even been told sociopaths have more imagination than normal people, so don't think you have to have an extraordinary imagination for it to be beneficial unless you desire to be anti-social.

If you frequently have bad dreams based on something that went on earlier in your life be sure to get some help, there is plenty out there that can help overcome these comebacks. Our life is too unique and valuable. God Bless and Sweet Dreams…

Now this short book is not about making you a great whatever or something else. My goal is to give you some thoughts and ideas to help build your self-esteem and self-image as well as deal with change.

If you really want to have good self-esteem and image it must be worked on all the time. Just like our attitude. I will go more into that shortly. All will help each of us feel better about ourselves as well as how others think of us. To this we must do actions that are good. That will be up to you.

Attitude Counts

Yes, attitude counts. I wrote a bit about the importance of attitude in my last book but thought we can go into it again in a different context. My first precept is what we all know. It is hard to keep a positive attitude all the time, especially as things seem to be difficult.

Give you an example, as I'm writing this the world and our wonderful country is dealing with a virus that has not only been deadly but has us doing things that are completely different than we have ever experienced. Things that we always thought as normal.

Our whole economy has been shut down, many have lost their good jobs and may never get them back. Here is where dealing with change becomes pertinent.

Put into quarantine for months, can't go to see our older family and friends, maintaining social distances. Can't even go to the beach, fly in an airplane, routinely go to a restaurant. Then comes professional, amateur, or school sports. All are a big part of American life.

Even my wife asked me as we were going into phase II of the quarantine, does that mean we get a new partner too?

PS that's a joke, at least I hope it is as I like being quarantined with her!

All are going to impact our normal life for a long, long time. Attitudes will and are being greatly impacted. Here is where having faith that we will adapt and eventually get over this comes into play.

Keep in mind Americans are free people and are amazing. We have come through many crippling catastrophes. As long as we are free, we will get through this current disaster.

Count Your Blessings

While our lives are going through difficulties, there are things we can do. First count our blessings. Attitude counts and blessings are a big part of maintaining positivity. This is especially true when everything seems upside down.

How do we count our blessings? Easy just make a list of them, keep them handy and as more come our way, add to our list.

The thing about the list is most of us are at a loss of where do we begin? How do we go about putting it together and what do we include?

Herc's a simple method. When you first make this list be sure you have quiet time. The object is not to be distracted.

Start by beginning with now and go backward in time. Go back in time as far as you want, don't worry about being too selective as every good thing, no matter how small, is a blessing. Using this method and going backward in time will help open our memory. Again, we do have an amazing brain.

A man once told me you never knew you have blessings until you count them. Make sense?

Have you done it yet, yes made that list? Probably not so it's a good time to get started.

Attitude

Here's another question for you, have you ever been around someone that seems to constantly have an attitude? You know what I mean: they are always complaining or are angry about something or other. Very seldom do they have a good word to say about anyone or anything, unless it's about themselves. Do we really appreciate their negativity?

What Comes Next?

Probably not and my suggestion is don't yourself take on this type of attitude as it most certainly will not help you to be the best you can be.

Think about it this way, many years ago Dr. Norman Vincent Peale wrote a book entitled *The Power of Positive Thinking*. It sold millions and even today is in almost every achievers library. Now here is another question, have you ever seen, read, or heard of a bestselling book based on the power of negative thinking? I think not!

Like what I discussed earlier in this book, here are a few suggestions for working on a positive attitude through the good times as well as the difficult times of our life.

- Work on it all the time.
- Hang around people with positive attitudes, both at work and outside of work. They are usually the happy, motivated types, if you get what I mean.
- Happy, satisfied, successful people are driven and can't afford to be around negative thinkers. Real leaders motivate others with a positive attitude. Some negative thinkers justify their attitudes by claiming to be contrarians. Don't believe them. They are just what they appear to be, negative thinkers. Stay away from them. They can be contagious just like covid. Maybe even more so, even a mask and social distancing won't help. Now it is okay to have real contrarian views. This can be accomplished and good come from them by using good questioning techniques. However, bashing every new idea or person that comes along is shallow.
- Negative attitudes create anger and depression. It's hard enough out there. We don't need more of it.
- Someone once told me to focus on the positives and you will have no time for the negatives. Remember that old song, "Accentuate the positive, eliminate the

negatives, latch on to the affirmative and don't mess with Mr. In Between..."

Enough said, let's move along.

Winners and Losers

It's about two boys that were walking down a country road when they came to a small freight loading platform on which were two milk cans, to be loaded for delivery in a nearby city.

The boys looked around and seeing no one, lifted the lid off the cover of can number 1 and dropped in a big bullfrog. Then they lifted the cover of can number 2 and dropped in another bullfrog. The boys continued down the country road., and later the cans were picked up and loaded for city delivery.

During the journey, the bullfrog in can number 1 said, "This is terrible. I can't lift the cover of the can because it's too heavy. I have never had a milk bath before, and I can't reach to the bottom of the can to get enough purchase to lift off the cover, so, what's the use." He gave up trying and quit.

When the cover of can number 1 was removed, there was a big dead bullfrog.

The same condition existed in can number 2, and the frog said to himself "Well, I can't lift off the cover, because it's too tight and heavy. I don't have a brace and bit to drill a hole to save myself, but by the great Father Neptune, there's one thing I learned to do in liquids and that is to swim. So, he swam and swam and swam and churned a lump of butter and sat on it. When the cover was lifted off, he jumped, hale and hearty, with the biggest broad jump ever recorded in frog history.

"The winner never quits, and the quitter never wins." (William E. Holler, Automotive Hall of Famer, motivational Speaker/Writer)

While that story may be off the theme of this book it certainly fits into what I'm trying to get across. Namely, use that amazing brain and be the best you can be.

Life Can Be Kind

While we are working on dealing with the challenges of dealing with change, self-esteem, and self-image, let's consider a few collaborative issues. One of them is the fact that occasionally life is kind and gives us what we want.

Most times however we work our butts off to get it. Is today one of those times? My suggestion is to decide what you want out of life. Then work for what you want.

Be careful what you wish for. Recently Dr. Thomas Sowells quoted a line from that infamous Nazi, Joseph Goebbels, "People will believe anything if it's repeated often enough and loud enough." He was probably right so be wary and look at what happened to the German people as well as the world.

Today as I write this it seems like we have let that old Egyptian camel's nose under our tent now. The Marxists/socialists, even the anarchists are trying to get the whole body of the camel into our tent (country). God forbid.

There are other factions that seem to have gained traction as well. Let's hope and pray our country remains free and civil rights of all as well as our laws are respected. Keep in mind that life is a mystery, and we will never know what comes next.

Part IV

The Stories of Joe Six-Pack

Joe Six-Pack

Recently a friend of mine shared some experiences over the course of his eventful life. Have included this section in my book as they say a lot about everyday life through the eyes of a variety of individuals.

In this case, the eyes of a young college student on his summer job as a toll collector on the San Francisco Bay bridge. I came to use this conveyance quite often while living in the bay area several years ago and wonder if maybe I fit into one or more of these categories? Hope not but, can't rule it out.

This friend by the name of John Pedroarena wrote this book while recovering from some heart related issues. He told me it was written for his kids, as he wanted them to experience some of the life lessons he had while becoming an adult. It was completed in 2014 and published on Amazon in 2018. You can purchase it from Amazon in e-book format.

I found these to be intriguing and John agreed to let me share a few of the stories with you. He wrote under the pseudonym Jack Pedro and entitled his book *Joe Six-Pack Bible for Survival, Comments from a Common Man* and is related to much included in this short book, including change, self-esteem and self-image. There are a lot of life lessons here especially relating to human nature and I know you will enjoy each and get his point.

Toll Collector

The first is called "my experience as a toll collector" and the mystery of being interrupted while driving. This involves the psychology of a driver's reaction when having to stop to pay a toll. As Joe Six-Pack (defined as the average man) opines it has something to do with the mesmerizing act of driving being interrupted.

This is where it gets interesting. In this scenario it is also me as Joe Sixpack. I had the graveyard shift from 10pm till 6 o'clock am on the Oakland-San Francisco Bay Bridge for one summer vacation. You are probably aware San Francisco is notorious for being a community of unusual individuals. Obviously, many of them used this bridge on a regular basis. You will meet some of them here.

After one of my stints, or about two weeks on the job, I wondered if either I was insane, or the world was. Before I go further, I still believe a student could write their PHD thesis on the psychology of driver's reactions while stopping to pay a toll. I now actually believe that it has to do with their act of driving being interrupted. Or maybe I was just the first person they talked to that day. Or perhaps they were just mean-spirited jackasses taking out their vengeance on me

One of the things I was told by my supervisor as I began my stint was eventually I was going to get robbed! Not maybe get robbed but robbed. As a 20-year-old, when I thought I was going to be robbed just figured I could handle it and maybe even be able to prevent it and be a hero.

Never considered that I could be killed in the process. Guess I was not only 20 years old but also naive! Fortunately, it never happened.

What Comes Next?

The things you see as a toll collector. During my graveyard shift about 3,000 cars and trucks passed through my booth, especially if I worked past 6 am and covered the morning shift. Not only is that a lot of vehicles, but you get to notice how people react to you as a person forcing them to stop and give you money.

Most handled the interruption well and most really didn't mind paying the toll. After all the only real alternative at the time before BART (Bay Area Rapid Transit) was to swim or drive South and go through San Jose and back up to San Francisco.

That thought did not enter the minds of most until I reminded them of that fact. When I did that, they mostly resented me and just thought, that wiseacre kid.

These comments about my experience on the Bridge may not do much for Joe Six-Pack but they are a commentary on people. Generally average people.

Here are a few examples of responses:

The Hot Coin Toss:

Some people just loved to heat the coins with their cigarette lighters and toss them at you. You really didn't burn your hand as the coins were not that hot, otherwise they would burn themselves. However, they were hot enough that the toll collector knew he was being screwed with. Guess some people just like to mess with what they see as the authority.

Big Brother Bothers Them:

Each day several people would stop and tell you, even if you didn't ask, that you should be ashamed of working for big brother government.

As I did wear a blue shirt and tie along with a hat, I did look as if I had authority. I remember a time when a van full of brothers gave me a hard time because I worked for the establishment, e. g. the oppressive government system that was the State of California. While a mild discussion incurred, when I told them I was just trying to make a living I think they understood. Maybe.

Directions Please:

This happened all the time with travelers asking me for directions. A frequent one was how do I get to the San Francisco Airport.? Well, it generally took no more than ten seconds and that's when the trailing cars became impatient. You know how that works with horns blowing when you take too long at a stop sign.

You knew there was a problem when the car asking for directions moved on but, the following car did not. Oh, its motor is revving but, and creeping forward as if the driver was positing himself to pay the toll. Ah, but alas that was too good to be true. Before you knew it, you had to expect the throw down to second and you had to be prepared to duck.

Yes, they would move their car forward rapidly as if to pay but would decide to throw the coin into your space instead of handing it to you.

You dropped quickly, retrieved the coin, uttered a few expletives, and waved the next car forward. No harm done unless the safety glass on the back side of the booth was cracked. Takes all kinds.

Germ Freaks:

As I said it takes all kinds. Now, many older folks won't touch your hand when they pass the toll coin. And this was long before the covid virus. Instead they would pass their coin using a clothes pin. Can you believe?

If I would have known about a worldwide germ exchange back then, I probably would have been paranoid. Today I believe they use latex gloves but, this was before then. The thing was while using the clothespin they avoided my germs, but I did not avoid theirs...

Yes, I Have No Money:

This was a frequent occurrence. Not everyone who travels through a toll booth is prepared to pay the toll. There are times I would cover for them if they acted kind and looked like they were really out of money. Sometimes we would have to stop traffic across all lanes to send the offending driver to headquarters in order that they could register their name and address so the State could send them a bill. Can you believe?

Fortunately, this was a rare occurrence, but it did happen.

Then there were the pretty young women that came through with no spare change. What to do she would ask? I would say you need to pay. On more than one occasion she would open her blouse and expose her girls and ask if that was enough payment? To me it was but not the Governor. So again, we would have to stop traffic and get her to headquarters before I made a fool of myself! Oh my, what a job.

The Con Man:

It takes all kinds but, there are plenty of these. Keep in mind that over 3,000 vehicles, both cars and trucks, pass by my booth, especially during a double shift. What I'm saying is that I would see all kinds. Here is one example, the driver of a truck would have to pay double because he was a commercial vehicle.

The con men types would approach the booth and start yapping hello and hand you one coin with the other hidden in his fist. When you called him on it, he would put up an argument that he wasn't a commercial vehicle, he was out of money and so on. You would give him that knowing look that he was wasting his time.

What Comes Next?

He would concede your point and hand over the second coin while of course looking away. No further eye contact from him. That's one of the secrets of a con - no eye contact.

The thing is he didn't know that I had seen it all before, the look, diverting eyes, just the overall body language. These traits told me a con was on the way before he even stopped.

Generally, these vehicles were not frequent users of the Bridge and thought I wouldn't notice or know the game.

From his perspective he was the superior adversary willing to draw and shoot before I had time to catch up.

What he failed to realize with the numbers of daily vehicles I was an expert quick draw artist, and he was only a school yard punk ready to be conned himself. Moral of this story don't try to con Wyatt Earp.

Authority Can Kill or at Least Maim:

I wore a police type hat with an insignia. Also, a dark blue shirt, dark tie, and dark pants.

A real look of authority.

I could tell that some of the travelers really paid attention when I spoke. Some may have even thought I was carrying a piece.

There were even times some drivers were so accommodating, submissive and attentive that I could have told them to stand on their heads naked and they would have done their best, then said, "Yes, Sir" and "Thank you, sir." That was scary. Maybe they were raised in a society or household where the authority figure set the rules.

Too bad, you cannot take advantage of those poor souls, but some collectors did. If they didn't speak English and they recognized their fear of the uniform, they could ask them to pay double or triple and sure enough they did. They kept the difference. I knew this happened on a regular basis. Too Bad.

What Comes Next?

My one clear memory of this authority fear came wrapped in the overpayment of a toll.

A woman in a station wagon who didn't speak English and was oblivious to where she was and why she had to pay a toll handed me a fist full of dollars as payment for a 25-cent toll. She had several young kids in the back portion of the wagon. A couple of the kids were in the backward facing rear seat. Of course, without seat belts.

When I politely said she overpaid her toll she continued to roll forward as if to leave.

Being an honest guy, I tried to get her attention by raising my voice over the adjacent din. How was I to know she was very responsive to the voice of authority as she immediately slammed on her brakes. With that the kids in the back flew over the seats ending up in the front seat all shook up. OUCH.

Authority may be one thing but, please lady don't endanger your kids just because some young punk tells you to stop.

Open for Business:

There are some perks working the graveyard shift way out away from the headquarters so you could be easily robbed or endangered.

Great way to spend your summer vacation.

But because of the graveyard sentence I became an enterprising entrepreneur in the way of commerce.

So, if you were robbed of quarters at least you had food and a newspaper to console yourself. This is how it worked.

Truckers and delivery men are great salt of the earth guys. Especially at 3 in the morning. They are the real Joe-Six Packs They are generous and love to mix it up in conversations.

Some of them would even try and trade themselves into a better feel good position. This is not a habit of truckers, everyone does it. What I mean is that many of us in life are stuck in the average Six-Pack positions regarding their jobs, money, status, family or whatever. We don't want to talk about it but, we know it down deep. So, we do what we do.

We bargain, swap, and talk and take a little advantage of the company the boss or whoever to try and equal out our lives. Guess that's just human nature. You know, just stick it to the man!

The drivers from the San Francisco Chronicle would be generous and give me a stack of the morning papers. The stack was freshly printed and still warm. Now this was 3am and they were on their way to the East Bay and beyond to the Central Valley. If the driver was lucky, the Carnation milk and butter driver had just passed my booth a few minutes before. If he did, papers were exchanged for a carton of milk. On subsequent days, the Carnation drivers were behind the Chronicle driver and they got the paper. On and on it went. From donuts to magazines to tickets to the auto show or even the Fillmore Auditorium to hear The Grateful Dead. The Fillmore gig never happened but, I always wish it had.

A veritable swap meet going on at 3:00 AM.

Next time you get up in the middle of the night, take comfort that commerce is transpiring at that moment. The world never sleeps.

For Entertainment Purposes (Or How to Experience Out of Norm Behavior):

Because you were invariably sent to the booth furthest away from the headquarters building (because you were the summer replacement) you often experienced those individuals who played fast and loose with their morals or behavior.

It was as if I'm a strange dude, and I need to stay out of the light. These are the ones that aimed for the booth furthest from the headquarters building. As a result, you saw all types in your booth. Things were happening in both the front and back seats of cars passing through. California is the land of fruits (as is in fruit cakes) and nuts. But I saw more apple coring and nut picking than I needed. Come to think of it I hope I washed my hands thoroughly after receiving coins from these characters.

Mister Ugly Has to be Ready to Rumble:

When you are a young college student, tall and considered somewhat good looking by only yourself, you can be easily offended when a toll payer before leaving says you are the ugliest guy on the face of the earth! Them thar are fighting words.

But you try to talk your way around by maybe saying that it was your parents' fault, not yours. Then hoping they would step on the accelerator and move along.

After All you had coins to gather for the Governor and you can't afford to yap at some idiot. Most move on, only sometimes they would get offended by your joke about their parentage.

Occasionally this would get serious and they would open their door as if to start a rumble. In this case you either shut their door on them or convinced them you had an arsenal in your booth that they didn't want to encounter. They usually got the point and generally moved on.

Probably most were either intoxicated, mean or crazy. Who knows?

These are a few of my summer job experiences as a toll collector. With so many momentary toll payer meetings during my shifts it is evident that the world is filled with all sorts. This experience opened my eyes to many of the Joe Six-Packs as well as the good, bad and the ugly.

For the most part ordinary citizens are like our neighbors, people we work with, etc. just human beings trying to live. Guess we all have different ideas on how this works. That is what makes America Great.

Here are some more comments from our Joe - SixPack (the average man) friend John Pedroarena. This one is called:

Brainwashing 101

Goes something like this. Recently had surgery and was holed up in the hospital for six days. With nothing else to do I watch a fair amount of television during my rehab. What is it about us humans that we must be told time and time again by the TV commercials to buy this product or drive that car? Maybe you will see the same commercial four times in one hour.

I realize the advertisers know we won't leave the football game and go right out and buy that high end, all powerful pick-up truck but, maybe something is guiding our subconscious when we go to the dealership next time to buy a vehicle.

Do we really need that truck or large SUV, or have we been brainwashed over months and years regarding what kind of wheels we should buy?

We normally do not want to be controlled by a young, upstart on Madison Avenue telling us what to buy.

If you came up to us in a bar and told us you could control our minds, there could well be some pushing and shoving to ensue. Just saying!

But has it already happened through the slow dribble of a mind controlling TV commercial?

Have they already set us up without knowing it? Yes, to desire an image or level of excitement expressed by the wheels we drive.

Are we such impressionable consumers that we easily buckle under these suggestive pressures? Maybe so...However maybe we subconsciously want to be manipulated and need these commercials to push us over the edge of buying what we wanted anyway.

Ok so we buy that truck or SUV, pay over $40,000 for it, and commit $600 per month for the next seven years while only getting 11 miles per gallon. What were we thinking? Well us "Joes" will justify it somehow even if we might be too embarrassed to say the truth. That is, we were sucked in!

We'll think of some good excuses like better safety for the wife and kids, four-wheeling at the push of a button or off roading that will never happen due to pressing needs of mowing the lawn or attending son's little league game.

We knew we would be able to justify it if we worked at it enough. Although the reason is probably hidden from view except for that view of our psyches visible only through the rear-view mirror.

Mind control and brainwashing obviously have a great deal of value to retail-oriented companies. That is why billions of dollars are spent every year on getting the most creative ads out to the public.

Just be aware of the potential mind control advertisers have over us Joe-Six Packs through television radio and social media. After all, we do have to think for ourselves at some time or other.

Denial

John Pedroarena has been so generous in supplying stories and observations from his book entitled *Joe Six-Pack's Bible for Survival, Comments from a Common Man*. He thought that the subject of Denial was perhaps a good fit for my ruminations on Change, Self-image, and Self-esteem. I likewise feel you would appreciate a short run through from Joe's standpoint of the average person.

Here we go and thanks John your words are well taken.

Denial. We all do it and we know we are doing it. We just can't seem to help ourselves because let's face it, we are human, weak, and imperfect.

We know one of our imperfections is the lack of strength here and there but look out if someone else recognizes our weaknesses and accuses us of doing or thinking wrong. We always want to protect our fragile egos and opinions of ourselves and so we lash out with denial, make plenty of excuses or look the other way.

Deep inside, where we don't want to look for fear of what will be found. We probably always know what will be found.

Hey Joe, just look inside when no one else is looking, peer over the edge into the darkness and get scared. Then stop turning away from the mirror.

When you do for one moment, you'll understand yourself a bit more. You may even become a bit humbler, which may lead to a little clarity in your psyche.

This in turn might make you realize us Joe Six-Packs are not perfect so we can accept ourselves a little more. We'll then spend less energy in the justification mode to others as well as ourselves. Being easier on us will help us survive our daily lives.

Our hopes with this book are to help deal with inevitable changes that come our way along with the people that help us to be the best we can be. Along the way, we will find our share of Joe Six-Packs and a host of others that fit different categories. All a part of life here in the USA.

Part V

Creating a Meaningful Life

What Comes Next?

Miracles

Do you believe in miracles? This is a little tidbit from one of my previous books. And I believe we need a few in these troubled times. By that I mean with the covid virus impacting and resulting in illness and fatalities across the country and the world. Along with many businesses shutting down, millions losing their jobs, social distancing, etc. then here in our country riots against those that put their lives on the line to protect our sorry souls. Heck people can't even go to their places of worship.

Miracles come all the time, generally they happen when most needed and the person has the faith and hope to believe they can occur. Most frequently it is almost at a time of hopelessness.

Maybe it's overcoming cancer, healing of a wound. Other times they are so innocuous that we don't even recognize them as miracles. Perhaps just consider it our good luck, good fortune even a coincidence in our favor. Let's just say they are small miracles or large miracles. Whatever they are they can get us back on track or lead to a change in our lives.

Moral being: Don't depend on a miracle to solve our dilemmas, just make good use of your God-given talents, have faith in your abilities and make changes when and where necessary.

Sounds simple but it's not so easy especially when we are facing a seamlessly hopeless situation. Our mind then takes another perspective. Almost like when we are seeing it from afar. What I mean is that it's easy to give advice when we are not involved but not so easy to give ourselves advice. Again, I say be careful and selective of who you trust with your actions.

What I mean is that doctors don't even understand the healing power of our bodies. They generally understand that by doing the right things there are powers at work that result in small and large unexplained miracles every day. Have you ever experienced where a so-called expert like a doctor gave you the wrong diagnosis or medication? Trust me it happens every day. Did you ever hear of the phrase, "Get a second opinion?"

Here's an example that relates in today's world with the virus claiming an impact on everyone. Can doctors explain how soap and water simply stops the virus while billions $$$$ are spent trying to find a vaccine? Doctors and scientists just don't know. Like I heard someone say a while ago, "Doctors treat, God cures."

Let's make it clear, when a vaccine is created through a myriad of trials and tests it generally will not cure existing cases. It will only hopefully end new cases, for those that are vaccinated. Existing cases will have to be treated by technology and cured by God. This is where miracles come from.

It's All About Life

I guess it's all about life. Seems we all, no matter how old, strive for more life. As all of us have a free will that provides us with many different expressions of how we live that life. That is how we each get most out of life.

Of course, some get more, some get less.

Let's get back to self-image again for a bit as it relates to life. Before that let's consider how old do we have to be until we feel our life is over as we are now worthless? Many years ago, it was when we retired. Often people even died a year or two after retiring. In fact, I believe that is how the Social Security tables were originally calculated. Never were people calculated to live as long as they do today. That is productive well into their 80's and even 90's.

Old Fogeys

If we are not desirous of leading a meaningful life after we retire, this can mean we are giving up on life and become an "old fogey." Yes, self-esteem goes by the wayside along with a myriad of life expressions. Many today never want to retire because they love what they do in their everyday activities. Do you know anybody in their 70's still working daily? Hell yes, I do know quite a few in fact. I'll bet you do too. And they generally are not doing it just for the money.

Think about what we all need, generally they are basic things like love, security, even creative expression (that is an active use of our amazing brain.) Even recognition helps as we all know babies cry for it and grown men die for it.

Looking Forward

Getting back to self-esteem, believe in yourself and look forward and not back. Oh, it's nice to reminisce especially with old friends from school, work or even time in the military but don't dwell on those times. When we stop being active, we probably become like that old fogey I mentioned earlier. As a suggestion consider venturing out, take a chance, try something new. Remember that bucket list?

Even my daughter when she had her 18th birthday (without telling her mom and dad) experienced a parachute jump. Her grandfather asked her, "You mean you jumped out of a perfectly good airplane?"

After all he had to bail out of a B24 bomber that was hit by Japanese anti-aircraft fire in the Pacific during World War II. As for me I was ticked she did such a thing as it had taken us a lot of time and money to get her to 18.

By the way, what's on your bucket list?

What comes next is difficult to predict at best. However, what we do as a person has a big influence on what happens in our own life. The ability to adapt to change, making the best of life as it occurs including good and bad will be a big influence on not only our self-image and self-esteem but, our levels of happiness and satisfaction.

As of this writing most of us have been holed up and stuck inside with the Covid virus as a threat. I'm sure we are all wondering what comes next. My suggestion is while the virus threat may come to a decent ending there will always be something next to contend with. Our self-esteem and self-image will enable us to survive and prosper.

We can be assured that we will get through it with our resolve and bold determination, maybe not be in the way we prefer but, that's life. Hope this writing gave you good insight and reasons to assess how you are dealing with everyday life.

Getting to know Mark Fierle

After graduating from Gannon University, Erie, Pa. he had a varied career in finance, marketing, and business management, working with large national and international firms.

Later he became President, CEO and Chairman of the Board of a large privately owned multi-state service company. From there it was the career field where after a few years he formed his own executive search firm. Along the way he began writing career-oriented articles as a freelance writer for a division of the Wall Street Journal. Along with his articles he was recognized as Consultant of the Year for the California Association of Personnel Consultants.

He was very successful in all his endeavors. Later he became a University of California trained

Master Gardener and Radio Talk Show Host on a program entitled "In the Garden."

This is his fourth inspirational book, beginning with a co-authored book, Adapt or Perish, based on the Darwinian theory of survival of the fittest and designed to help businesses survive in the era of change and social media.

Next it was Rekindling the American Dream that included strategies and tactics to help us all restore hope during the great recession of the Obama era.

His third book is Unbridling the American Spirit and was designed to provide inspiration for us to lead a meaningful life, overcoming the tendencies of the "entitlement" society. This included the four building blocks of a meaningful life from Mark's point of view.

All are available in both e-book and soft cover formats on Amazon. All are rated five stars.

Mark has now lives in Texas and most of this book was written with a Texas accent, so be aware.

www.ingramcontent.com/pod-product-compliance
Lightning Source LLC
Chambersburg PA
CBHW071017040426
42443CB00007B/814